Scot's Songs

Allan Ramsay

In the interest of creating a more extensive selection of rare historical book reprints, we have chosen to reproduce this title even though it may possibly have occasional imperfections such as missing and blurred pages, missing text, poor pictures, markings, dark backgrounds and other reproduction issues beyond our control. Because this work is culturally important, we have made it available as a part of our commitment to protecting, preserving and promoting the world's literature. Thank you for your understanding.

SCOTS SONGS.

By Allan Ramsay.

𝕮𝖍𝖊 𝕾𝖊𝖈𝖔𝖓𝖉 𝕰𝖉𝖎𝖙𝖎𝖔𝖓.

EDINBURGH:
Printed for the Author at the *Mercury*, opposite to *Niddrey*'s-Wynd, 1719.

SCOTS SONGS

The happy Lover's Reflections.

I.

THE last Time I came o'er the Moor
I left my Love behind me;
Ye Pow'rs! What Pain do I endure
when soft Ideas mind me?
Soon as the ruddy Morn display'd
the beaming Day ensuing,
I met betimes my lovely MAID,
in fit Retreats for wooing.

II.

Beneath the cooling Shade we lay
gazing, and chastly sporting;
We kiss'd and promis'd Time away,
till Night spread her black Curtain:

I pitied all beneath the Skies,
   ev'n Kings, when she was nigh me,
In Raptures I beheld her Eyes,
   which could but ill deny me.

III.

Shou'd I be call'd where Cannons roar,
   where mortal Steel may wound me,
Or cast upon some foreign Shore,
   where Dangers may surround me,
Yet Hopes again to see my Love,
   to feast on glowing Kisses,
Shall make my Cares at Distance move,
   in Prospect of such Blisses.

IV.

In all my Soul there's not one Place
   to let a Rival enter;
Since she excells in ev'ry Grace,
   in her my Love shall center.
Sooner the Seas shall cease to flow,
   their Waves the *Alps* shall cover;
On *Greenland* Ice shall Roses grow,
   before I cease to love her.

V. The

V.

The next Time I go o'er the Moor
   she shall a Lover find me,
And that my Faith is firm and pure,
   tho' I left her behind me:
Then *Hymen*'s sacred Bonds shall chain
   my Heart to her fair Bosom,
There while my Being does remain,
   my Love more fresh shall blossom.

The Lass of Peattie's *Mill.*

I.

THE Lass of *Peattie*'s Mill,
   So bonny, blyth and gay,
In spite of all my Skill,
She stole my Heart away.
When tedding of the Hay
Bare-headed on the Green,
Love 'midst her Locks did play,
And wanton'd in her Een.

II.

Her Arms white, round and smooth,
Breasts rising in their Dawn,
To Age it wou'd give Youth,
To press 'em with his Hand.
Thro' all my Spirits ran
An Extasy of Bliss,
When I such Sweetness fand
Wrapt in a balmy Kiss.

III.

Without the Help of Art,
Like Flowers which grace the Wild,
She did her Sweets impart,
When e'er she spoke or smil'd.
Her Looks they were so mild,
Free from affected Pride,
She me to Love beguil'd,
I wish'd her for my Bride.

IV.

O had I all that Wealth
Hopetoun's high Mountains fill,
Insur'd long Life and Health,
And Pleasures at my Will;

I'd promise and fulfill,
That none but bonny She,
The Lass of *Peattie*'s Mill
Shou'd share the same wi' me.

DELIA,

To the Tune of Green Sleeves.

I.

YE watchful Guardians of the FAIR
   Who skiff on Wings of ambient Air,
Of my dear DELIA take a Care,
   and represent her Lover
With all the Gayety of Youth,
With Honour, Justice, Love and Truth,
'Till I return, her Passions sooth
   for me, in Whispers move her.

II.

Be careful no base sordid Slave,
With Soul sunk in a Golden Grave,
Who knows no Virtue but to save,
   with glaring Gold bewitch her.

Tell

Tell her for me she was design'd,
For me who know how to be kind,
And have more Plenty in my Mind,
 than one who's ten Times richer.

III.

Let all the World turn upside down,
And Fools run an eternal Round,
In Quest of what can ne'er be found,
 to please their vain Ambition.
Let little Minds great Charms espy
In Shadows which at Distance ly,
Whose hop'd for Pleasures when come nigh
 prove nothing in Fruition.

IV.

But cast into a Mold Divine,
Fair *DELIA* does with Lustre shine,
Her virtuous Soul's an ample Mine,
 which yields a constant Treasure.
Let POETS in sublimest Lays,
Imploy their Skill her Fame to raise;
Let Sons of MUSICK pass whole Days,
 with well tun'd Reeds to please her.

The Yellow-hair'd Laddie.

I.

IN *April* when Primroses paint the sweet Plain,
And Summer approaching rejoiceth the Swain,
The *Yellow-hair'd Laddie* would oftentimes go
To Wilds and deep Glens where the Hawthorn trees grow.

II.

THERE under the Shade of an old sacred Thorn,
With Freedom he sung his Loves Ev'ning and Morn:
He sung with so soft and inchanting a Sound,
That *Silvans* and *Fairies* unseen danc'd around.

III.

THE Shepherd thus sung, Tho young *MAYA* be fair,
Her Beauty is dash'd with a scornful proud Air;
But *SUSIE* was handsome and sweetly could sing,
Her Breath like the Breezes perfum'd in the Spring.

IV.

THAT *MADIE* in all the gay Bloom of her Youth
Like the Moon was unconstant and never spoke Truth;
But *SUSIE* was faithful, good humour'd and free,
And fair as the Goddess who sprung from the Sea.

V.

THAT Mamma's fine Daughter, with all her great dowr,
Was aukwardly airy, and frequently sowr.
Then sighing he wished, would Parents agree,
The witty sweet *SUSIE* his Mistress might be.

NAN-

[10]

NANNY O.

I.

WHILE some for Pleasure pawn their Health
'Twixt *Lais* and the *Bagnio*,
I'll save my self and without Stealth
Kiss and caress my NANNY---O.
She bids more fair t' ingage a *JOVE*
Than *LEDA* did, or *DANAE*---O,
Were I to paint the QUEEN of LOVE,
None else shou'd sit but NANNY---O.

II.

'HOW joyfully my Spirits rise,
When dancing she moves finely---O,
I guess what Heaven is by her Eyes,
Which sparkle so divinely---O:
Attend my Vow, ye Gods, while I
Breath in the blest *BRITANNIO*,
None's Happiness I shall envy,
As long's ye grant me NANNY---O.

Chorus.

My bonny, bonny NANNY---O,
My lovely charming NANNY---O,
I care not tho the World know
How dearly I love NANNY---O.

Bonny JEAN.

I.

LOVE's Goddess in a Myrtle Grove
Said, *CUPID*, bend thy Bow with speed,
Nor let the Shaft at random rove,
For *JEANIE*'s haughty heart must bleed.
The smiling Boy, with divine Art,
From *Paphos* shot an Arrow keen,
Which flew unerring to the Heart,
And kill'd the Pride of bonny *JEAN*.

II.

NO more the Nymph, with haughty Air,
Refuses *WILLIE*'s kind Address,
Her yielding Blushes shew no Care,
But too much Fondness to suppress.
No more the Youth is sullen now,
But looks the gayest on the Green,
Whilst every Day he spies some new
Surprising Charms in bonny *JEAN*.

III.

A Thousand Transports crowd his Breast,
He moves as light as fleeting Wind,
His former Sorrows seem a Jest,
Now when his *JEANIE* is turn'd kind:
Riches he looks on with Disdain,
The glorious Fields of War look mean;
The chearful Hound and Horn give Pain,
If absent from his bonny *JEAN*.

IV.

THE Day he spends in am'rous Gaze,
Which even in Summer shorten'd seems,
When sunk in Downs with glad Amaze,
He wonders at her in his Dreams.
All Charms disclos'd she looks more bright
Than *Troy*'s Prize the *Spartan* Queen,
With breaking Day he lifts his Sight,
And pants to be with bonny *JEAN*.

The Kind Reception,

To the Tune of Auld lang syne.

I.

SHOULD auld Acquaintance be forgot,
    tho' they return with Scars?
These are the noble HEROE's Lot,
    obtain'd in glorious Wars:
Welcome my *VARO* to my Breast,
    thy Arms about me twine,
And make me once again as blest,
    as I was lang syne.

II.

Methinks around us on each Bough
    a Thousand *Cupids* play,
Whilst thro' the Groves I walk with you
    each Object makes me gay.
Since your Return the Sun and Moon
    with brighter Beams do shine,
Streams murmure soft Notes while they run,
    as they did lang syne.

III.

Despise the Court and Din of State,
  let that to their Share fall.
Who can esteem such Slav'ry great,
  while bounded like a Bal?
But sunk in Love, upon my Arms
  let your brave Head recline,
We'll please our selves with mutual Charms,
  as we did lang syne.

IV.

O'er Moor and Dale with your gay Friend
  you may pursue the Chace,
And after a blyth Bottle end
  all Cares in my Embraces.
And in a vacant rainy Day
  you shall be wholly mine;
We'll make the Hours run smooth away,
  and laugh at lang syne.

V.

The HEROE pleas'd with the sweet Air
  and Signs of gen'rous Love
Which had been utter'd by the FAIR,
  bow'd to the POW'RS above:

Next Day with Consent and glad Haste
   th' approach'd the sacred Shrine,
Where the good Priest the Couple blest,
   and put them out of Pine.

The PENITENT,

To the Tune of the Lass of *Livingston.*

I.

PAIN'D with her slighting *JAMIE*'s Love,
   BELL dropt a Tear,— *BELL* dropt a Tear,
The Gods descended from above,
   Well pleas'd to hear, — Well pleas'd to hear;
They heard the Praises of the Youth
   From her own Tongue, — From her own Tongue,
Who now converted was to Truth,
   And thus she sung, — And thus she sung.

II.

Blest Days when our ingen'ous Sex,
   More frank and kind, — More frank and kind,
Did not their lov'd Adorers vex,
   But spoke their Mind, — But spoke their Mind:

Repenting now she promis'd fair
Wou'd he return, — Wou'd he return,
She ne'er again wou'd give him Care,
Or cause him mourn, — Or cause him mourn.

III.

Why lov'd I the deserving SWAIN,
Yet still thought Shame, — Yet still thought Shame,
When he my yielding Heart did gain,
To own my Flame, — To own my Flame?
Why took I Pleasure to torment,
And seem too coy, — and seem too coy,
Which makes me now alas lament,
My slighted Joy, — My slighted Joy?

IV.

Ye FAIR, while Beauty's in its Spring,
Own your Desire, — Own your Desire;
While Love's young Power with his soft Wing
Fans up the Fire, — Fans up the Fire;
O do not with a silly Pride,
Or low Design, — Or low Design,
Refuse to be a happy Bride,
But answer plain, — But answer plain.

V.

Thus the FAIR MORUNER wail'd her Crime,
With flowing Eyes, — With flowing Eyes,
Glad *JAMIE* heard her all the Time,
With sweet Surprise: — With sweet Surprise:
Some God had led him to the Grove,
His Mind unchang'd, — His Mind unchang'd
Flew to her Arms, and cry'd my Love,
I am reveng'd! — I am reveng'd!

LOVE's CURE.

To the Tune of Peggy I must love thee.

I.

AS from a Rock past all Relief,
   the shipwrackt *COLIN* spying
His native Home, o'ercome with Grief,
   half sunk in Waves and dying;
With the next Morning Sun he spies
A Ship, which gives unhop'd Surprise,
New Life springs up, he lifts his Eyes
   with Joy, and waits her Motion:

II.

So when by her whom long I lov'd,
   I scorn'd was and deserted,
Low with Despair my Spirits mov'd
   to be for ever parted;
Thus droopt I till diviner Grace
I found in *PEGGY*'s Mind and Face,
Ungratitude appear'd then base,
   but Virtue more engaging.

III.

Then now since happily I've hit,
   I'll have no more delaying,
Let Beauty yield to manly Wit.
   we lose our selves in staying;
I'll haste dull Courtship to a Close,
Since Marriage can my Fears oppose,
Why should we happy Minutes lose,
   since *PEGGY* I must love thee?

IV.

Men may be foolish if they please,
   and deem't a Lover's Duty
To sigh, and sacrifice their Ease,
   doating on a proud Beauty:
Such was my Case for many a Year,
Still Hope succeeding to my Fear,
False *BETTY*'s Charms now disappear,
   since *PEGGY*'s far outshine them.

ODE.

HENCE every Thing that can
Disturb the Quiet of Man,
   Be blyth my Soul,
   In a full Bowl
     Drown thy Care,
     And repair
The vital Stream;
Since Life's a Dream,
Let Wine abound,
And Healths go round,
We'll sleep more sound,
And let the dull unthinking Mob pursue
Each endless Wish, and still their Toil renew.

Printed by Libri Plureos GmbH in Hamburg, Germany